Scribbles, Rhymes, and Lima Beans

poems that grow on you

Rachael Waldburger

ROSEDENE PUBLISHING

MERRILL , WISCONSIN

For Mom,
who taught me how to plant
peonies and poems.

CONTENTS

Author's Note

These poems are arranged into three sections:

Scribbles features poems about life and love.
Rhymes features poems about writing, art, and inspiration.
Lima Beans features poems about growth and renewal.

Scribbles

The Wall

The wall was built in '92.
It started small, and then it grew.
And snow and rain and hail endured,
and bore it all
as walls must do.

Lying on My Back in October

The leaves look like potato chips,
they sound like fresh potato chips
against the ceiling, bright and crisp,
the lightest, bluest sky.
Not a cloud goes by
and I
sigh.
The grass smells green
and clean between
my toes.
I watch; it grows.
I grow, too
slow, up to
the blue.
Not a clue
how I'll get down
back to the ground
where I have found
a place to lay
and waste away
a quiet day.
The tree branch sways
and feather-soft
from where, aloft,
the leaf had been,
I sink again.
I feel the Earth spin
beneath me.

Raspberries

Raspberries taste better
fresh from Grandma's garden
sun warm and slightly squashed
from being dropped into
repurposed ice cream buckets
(hanging from a shoe string
tied around your waist)
all sticky on your fingers.

They taste better when
you scratch your hands
bending back the leaves and stems,
hunting for the hidden patches
Grandpa missed that morning.

They taste better when
you line up your buckets on the kitchen table
and pour your berries into a cereal bowl
with milk and sprinkled sugar.

They taste better
in my memory, where
the farm still belongs to Grandpa and Grandma,
where the barn still stands
and the raspberries still grow.

Running

I
run
to feel
my legs burn.
I fall to
feel
the grass and
smell
the dirt.
I climb
to jump
and land
undignified.
I climb again
to jump
and touch the sky.

Old Crush

You happen upon my daydreams now and again,
　　　　passing through
　　　　as I go about my day,
when the hours are long
and the years stretch on
and I begin to wonder if
daydream love
is all I'll ever know.
There is no pressure to our meetings,
　　　　no longing or loneliness.
　　　　Just the reminder that
love exists,
in passing and in memory
and in hope.
You always seem to wander past
　　　　when the flame is lowest.

Argument

I am a formidable foe in the guise of a girl.

I am calm and cool, composed, a cat
I am a tiger, tireless, that
stares down my enemy, amber-eyed,
(hiding the streaks of the tears I have cried
in the boldly-marked stripes on the bridge of my nose).
Every word spoken in rage to me goes
with the swiftness of prey to my razor-sharp claws,
and then with a leap to my bone-crushing jaws.
I snatch out the message and swallow it whole,
though the acid within it is death to the soul.
I savor the lesson, consider the words
and then leave between us the bones for the birds.

Realization

I don't owe my life to you;
it's not a debt I need to spend
paying back with interest.
A child is not a sculpture that
you get to mold the way you want.
I am a masterpiece of a design
far beyond your grasp, and I
do not owe my life to you.

Wild–Grown

You took us out into the wilds
and left us to the weather
and the wolves.

I wound my way
along forest trails,
until I found the sunlight again.

He learned to bear his fangs
in protection
instead of fear.

We grew,
not thanks to,
but in spite of you.

Wolf

You can't be upset
when you throw a boy to the wolves
and he learns to bite back.

Sometimes

Sometimes when I try to remember
the struggles of my childhood,
the warmth of
her arms around me
and a book in her hands
chases the pain away.

Reflections

She hands me a book,
Reflections on a Gift of Watermelon Pickle

and I glimpse the girl she used to be
in the gleam of the cover.

She reads me the words
without looking at the pages.

It's like going back in time
and forward in time

to a moment when we are both
fearless dreamers.

Boxes

I like to put things in boxes:
bills in one, mail in another,
plans for the future, receipts,
memories and pain
all in their own little spaces,
packed neatly away,
some tied together with strings,
some with chains.

Falling(inlove)

There's a reason they call it "falling"
in love.   If you've never fallen
from a substantial height,
it's hard to understand.
It's terrifying.
                Your stomach drops
away and your blood turns
cold and your lungs forget how
to breathe. Your mind
can only think *make it*
stop make it stop make it stop
and you try to find something
to brace yourself against
but there's nothing.
Time is simultaneously
quickened

and

slowed;

40 seconds seems like
40 years,   but
when it's over you can hardly believe
how short it was.

Your brain was so preoccupied with survival
that you can't recall many details,
but the ones you do remember
make you think,
"Well.
        That wasn't
        so
        bad."

I Think He Thinks in Music

I think he thinks in music
and I am just a poem.
He's always singing,
and even when he's not, there's
music in his movements.
While I, preoccupied
as I am with the lyrics,
am constantly missing steps.
Words are easy, are
syllables and rhythms and
definitions, definite.
Not music.
It's free and
unstructured and
dangerous
because
a song without words is still beautiful,
but what are lyrics without a tune?

You Would Be

You would be
my adventure,

my shelter, my
knight in dented armor.

You would warm the
cold, dark

places of my heart,
would smooth the roughened edges,

mend the jagged tears
and when I shrink back,

would take my hands
and tell me not to go.

It would be so
if I were brave

enough to let you in.

Would You Look For Me

If you and I were
stories in a book,
would you take the time to look
for me in pages aged
and tearing, tucked between
the smooth-spined
thin and oft-read
stories of our time?
Would you stand
on tippy-toes and reach your hand
above the squeaking,
loudly speaking
conquest-seeking books
would you look
for me in silence?
Would you read
beyond my cover, would you
wait for me to open,
coax a smile and
set me hoping for
something different, something more
than all I've ever known
and now that I am grown
past the need for hiding in my books,
would you let me look
beside you
for our fairytale?

Smitten

You doubt I've been smitten
I haven't yet written
a poem declaring love.
I doubt I could do it,
I've never gone through it,
this thing you're thinking of.

My words are a-flutter,
my heartbeat a stutter,
my thoughts won't settle still;
each butterfly lingers
whenever his fingers
play music on my will.

A melody soaring,
this fire set roaring
whenever we're alone.
We're hearts of a feather,
so how could I tether
such feelings to a poem?

Knight Errant

All these years worrying for
my knight errant, and,
errant myself, never realizing
now crucial it is
to wait.

Tilting at Windmills

The blessing of
the years between us
is that I never had to watch
my knight errant tilt
against windmills,
and he never saw me
cower from mine.

Death Waited Patiently His Turn

Death waited patiently His turn
and we with Him in the sterile white room.
We knew it was time, and we were all ready
and not ready to let him go.

He was 93, and his strength had turned inward
and sleep claimed his time and his hearing had gone.
It was hard to see such a
man like that, and we were not ready
and ready to let him go.

His stubbornness had held Death at bay
two or three times before,
so that even now He hesitated to act,
expecting a fight.

But then amid the silence and white,
from the doorway came laughter and faltering steps
and into the room filled with waiting and dying
the toddler came tumbling in.

Death, almost ready to reach out his hand,
gave pause to the child and considered,
and looked at the bed and remembered a time
when the hands resting wrinkled and work-worn
had been clumsy and reaching and new.

He smiled at the child, let the laughter continue,
and looked on, enchanted, as seldom he is.
And when the time came, at last we were ready
and not ready to let him go.

Hard to Be Sad

It's hard to be sad
when I know she was ready;
she said she was ready
and wanted to go.
It's hard to be sad
when her memory was jumbled,
she knew she'd forgotten,
she wanted to know.
It's hard to be sad
when I know she was hurting,
I know she was missing
the ones gone before;
but it's hard to be anything
else at the moment,
so sad I will be
for a little while more.

Grandpa's Jacket

At the foot of his grave,
I bury my hands
in borrowed pockets,
hoping for spare
wisdom.

Empty Seats

How is it that
surrounded by my family
on the happiest day of my life,
all I can think about is
the empty seats?

Rhymes

To All The Unknown Poets

To all the unknown poets of the world
who work in anonymity and cast
their queries and submissions to the void
where even echoes make a rare reply,
who, gazing at the stars above their reach,
make rockets from voracity and verse

would that the world could read the tales we tell,
could catch each falling star before it fell.

Rebel

When I was in 3rd grade
my teacher introduced us to Poetry
and I noticed that
not every line
had a period.

I raised my hand,
triumphant, having
found an error in the book.

"It's not wrong,"
said Mrs. Klug.
"Poets don't have to follow the rules."
And unintentionally, she
cemented in my mind
the desire to be a
punctuation rebel.

Pink

Pink was my favorite color
until I turned eight
and the boys made it clear that
pink meant
weakness.
> Pink was Girly
> and Girly was
> contemptible.
So I renounced the color
and all it stood for
and became a Tomboy.
It wasn't as good as
being a real boy,
but it was acceptable.
I fell into the lie that
I wasn't like Other Girls,
dramatic and vapid and
obsessed with my looks.
> I didn't know any girls like this
> but apparently they just weren't
> Other Girls either.
I learned that I liked
football and swordfights,
pirates and pioneers,
and that those things are incompatible
with pink.
> I learned that I liked
> flowers and poetry,
> kittens and cooking,
> and that I could only enjoy them with
> Mom or Grandma.

I learned that I had to be stronger than,
smarter than,
better than
if I was going to be
anything at all.
I learned that I had to
speak up
        but not over him
dress up
        to his liking
make up
        when he was wrong
give up
        if he wanted it
shut up
        when he spoke
grow up
on my own experiences
and the drive of the women before me
who had learned that Other Girls
were just as tired as I was
of pretending they didn't
        like pink.

Masterpiece

Orion's Belt is spread
in freckles on my arm,
and beneath my right ring finger is
a scar shaped like a heart.
Beside my left eye is a
beauty mark any 17th century
French aristocrat would envy,
and my fingers, my mother said
when I was a baby,
destined me to be either a
pianist or a pickpocket.
Details more intricate
than any master painting,
planned and placed with
meticulous devotion
by the Creator Himself.
And you want to convince me that I
am ugly.

Inside

The people sit
inside the room.
They talk, debate,
          attack, assume.
They plan and plot,
          they pluck and prune.
They stand; the meeting's
ending soon
and they have things
to do.

No one sees
that through the glass
          are flowers, trees,
          are rocks and grass.
No one knows
and no one asks

the people simply
pass.

Ode to Gladys (Rembrandt's *Girl at a Window*)

I wonder as I critique
your too-dark eyes,
your too-bright lips,
your too-pale face,
if I wasn't meant
to choose you.
I picked you because
you had an easy background.
Blobby shadows
(a desk
or a windowsill
or a bucket/curtain/cornerstone
thing)
and you.
I wanted to challenge myself
with something I'd never
painted before.
A face,
folded cloth.
But now I wonder
if I was never meant for you.
After a week,
you're still not done.
I keep going back to
the parts I've already finished,
reworking, replacing, regretting.
I'm not sure what I'm doing
and it shows.
You stare at me,
irreversible.

You watch me laugh
at you,
cry
for you,
pull my hair out
because of you.
I make up your story,
tell it,
forget it,
improvise.
Are you teaching me something?
Giving me a lesson that
can only be learned
through hardship?
Or laughing at me
with the too-dark eyes
and the too-bright lips
        that I gave you?

Inspiration

I felt it when I woke this morning;
skies were gray and soaked with rain.
Deep within, the pool sent ripples
dancing to my thoughts again.
Frost has covered dormant water,
settled in its watchful sleep.
Why it wakes I cannot fathom,
cannot pierce the gathered deep.
I have learned to wait with patience,
learned to drink with shallow sips,
learned to savor when it leaves me
with a poem on my lips.

Ninja

I never realized until
today that I had ninja skill.
My glass fell from the windowsill
and I, with massive power of will,
wishing not my glass to kill,
snatched it up with moves so chill
that not a drop from it did spill.
This action did my ego fill,
for I am gloating of it still.

Charlie

Charlie the White Knight,
out riding one bright night
to make his final stand,
cried, "Hey Diddle Diddle,"
his thumbs all a–twiddle,
a poem on his hand.
He spun like a beetle
the black compass needle,
and watched the dragon fly,
to the tics and the tocks
of the dual dueling clocks,
at opposite ends of the sky.
But the dragon flew out
without challenge or doubt,
its hordes and herds to steal.
And to battle alone
armed with only a poem
is a pain even words cannot heal.

I Am a Poem

I am a poem,
structured and sure,
you know what I tell you,
you know nothing more.

I have a meaning,
more than what seems.
I speak in riddles,
I speak in dreams.

I am a secret,
I am your friend.
Read me more slowly,
read me again.

How to Write a Poem

Pick a memory and
squeeze until
words come out.

Writer's Block

Apparently no poems today.
My pen will not write
what I want to say.

New Project

No journey is as daunting
as paper new and white.
No voyage as disheartening
as words that don't fit right.
No trek is as discouraging
as hands that idle sit,
if ever there was such a poem,
good reader, this is it.

Words

Words are jagged, double-edged betrayers.
They are treacherous,
dangerous
the worst of all traitors
because
they make you trust them,
and you go down knowing they deserted you;
you cling to them anyway.
They infect you
and become part of you
until there is no more distinction,
until the "you" that was before
is only a shadow,
irretrievable.
Words make you want things:
love and adventure and
things you can never have.
Things you know you can never be.
And there is no cure
and if there was
you wouldn't take it anyway.

Fairy Tales

There is a reason we tell ourselves
fairy tales.
I used to think
it was for the adventure, then
for the hope, then
for the love.
But in the darkest hour,
when despair sets in,
when the hero fails and
love is lost and
friends forsake and shadows grip the pages
always, there is the
pulsing of a story
that must continue.
Whether toward victory or failure,
love or loss,
there is a reason
we tell ourselves
fairy tales.

Poetry Purrs

in my ear like a cat
on my lap, soothing,
sensing distress,
heartache, and
curls around me,
comforting, kneading
paws and pauses
to rub soft fur
and free verse
against my hand
and asks for nothing in return
but my attention.

To Kill a Mockingbird

Evening is cornfields and sunflowers,
and Johnny Cash singing at sunset,
laughter and an open highway
and a tank full of gas.
The world is a gilded sepia
photograph of better times, and
I have a borrowed book that speaks
in a voice I used to play
on repeat in my head.
The proof of his love
is in the creased spine, the bent pages;
abused by affection.
I turn the page and
the summer air cools,
the sky darkens,
and his voice fades away,
and the sun sinks behind the words.
I can only read them once before
they too become a memory.

My Heart Would Wander

My heart would wander all forlorn
if ever I would let it,
but no one ever asked for love
who did not soon regret it.

Old Aker Kirke

At Old Aker Kirke
at half past eight,
a man puts a rose
in the old iron gate.
He does not pause,
he does not wait,
does not look back,
cannot be late.

The city wakes,
the sidewalks fill,
and Oslo hums;
the rose is still.

At Old Aker Kirke
at half past four,
the man walks by
the old church door.
The rose is gone
like the day before,
like it will be tomorrow,
and evermore.

A Dripping January Mist

A dripping January mist
dampens my hood and my mood.
I shield my eyes, blinding
myself as the diamond dust settles
on street lamp–lit roads
and packed stacks of snow.

A scattering of jewels
that nobody sees.

March

March craves green
along the stream
of consciousness that flows

from lines on white
fresh paper bright
where artists will suppose.

But only gray
has filled the day
from Lenten hymns all slow

and skies that cloud
above a shroud
of ashen, dirty snow.

Sometimes I Write

"Sometimes I write,"
he says,
shrugging like
it's no big deal,
but watching for
my admiration.

"Sometimes I write,"
I answer,
the way I'd say
"Sometimes I breathe."

Critique

"Don't be afraid to tackle
the difficult questions,"
he says, the wise professor
to his underling.
"Where is the darkness, the mess,
the hard truth?
Show us the pain and the struggle.
Not everyone's life is all
sunshine and gardens."

(This with a glance at my
lavender-printed
sketching-drenched notebook
and summer-green pen.)

If only he knew
the thorns in this garden,
the pages I carved
instead of the skin.
The rot in the roots and the
ink stains that blossomed
from shallow spilled soil
and sunflower seeds.

I don't wear my pain
in the books that I carry
or the words that I choose to explain.
So I tell him, "The Renaissance painters
made darkness a background.
The focus is always
the figure in light.
I do the same, because life is as true
in the sunshine as in the shadows."

Emily Dickinson

he says there is no
purpose for
artistic liberties.

we do not know
what's wall or door,
truth or similes.

no purpose, so
intentions are
mere disabilities

I would not speak
assumptions, nor
compare the wind and breeze

Waterfalls

I have drunk from waterfalls
in Colorado, Tennessee,
Norwegian mountains
and Midwest creeks, and
each one tasted
like a time before
water treatment plants,
before paved trails
leading into valleys,
before roads cut through the land.
They say time travel is science fiction;
I say hike a mountain
and drink from waterfalls.

Upon Reaching the End

I can only blame myself.
The dread, the pain,
slightly different yet the same.
The fleeting glimpse of joy was
temporary, I knew.
Knew it all along,
knew it couldn't last,
knew that it would burn
and choke and tear apart
my silly, hopeful heart
knew that time was limited, even from the start.
I wish my path had never crossed
the book my cousin lent me.

Lima Beans

Adulting

I learned to think and contemplate,
I learned what's right and true.
I learned to study and to know,
I never learned to do.

Bar Harbor, Maine

I wake before the sun when still the sky is dark,
when masts upon the harbor rise like bare-leaved autumn
trees
back home, a thousand miles and miracles away
from this, the first horizon touched by morning's promise.

I wake before the first alarms I set,
to prompt me out of bed so I can greet the sun
beside my husband, who has roused against his will
to sit in silence on the deck, our shadows stretched behind us.

I wake before the harbor bells have tolled
their call to sailors, and to those of us who haven't
had a chance to find our sea legs, but whose ears
recall the ocean's sounding in the pounding of our pulse.

I wake before the sunrise with echoes in my ears,
the Midwest harbor bell's equivalent, a train's
faint whistle, calling me to rise, to follow
out over the tracks, the sun's gold light across the waves.

Spring

Spring starts gray
skies holding their heavy
sulking clouds, sprinkling
storms that weep and rage.

Green is the later
goal, the plunder stolen, ill-
gotten gains we hoard and
gather in verse and song.

Spring is not a
gentle waking up, it is a
swift war raged between
generations of frost and flora.

Fernweh

Certain days are just
driving, or
wanting to.
When the sun gleams
like polished armor,
dazzled, dream-glossed
wide-awake imagination,
so that even in the snow, it says,
"Cast off your coat,
leave everything
and go."
And even though it's cold
you *know* it is
the people outside breathe dragon-breath clouds
all you can think is
"Where are my keys?"
You have a full tank
and if there were no obligations
life would be perfect.

Waiting by the Fire

My friend has gone to feed cats,
my love is far away,
and I am sitting by the fire
with naught to do but pray.
I thank You for the firelight,
I thank You for the stars,
for all the gifts that come and go,
for all we think is ours.
The night is cold, the autumn chill,
but I've my daily bread.
Let smoke rise up like incense, Lord,
with hymns sung in my head.

First House

This is the house I did not want
to admit I wanted,
but as always, my prayer was answered
not the way I prayed,
but the way I needed.
The offer was made and accepted,
and the house was ours.
There was so much pressure and
rushed emails, phone calls,
documents to sign,
and then packing and
the move in two days and
cleaning the apartment
I wanted you to be excited,
but every time we walked through
you found more things we had to fix,
and I worried you regretted our decision.
But once we began to settle into ourselves again,
you said it was growing on you.
I didn't tell you
about the visions I could see:
a crib in the little bedroom,
a bed with dinosaur sheets,
tiny shoes on the front mat,
homework at the kitchen table.
I see us sitting outside and
listening to the radio, watching
the bats swoop overhead.
I picture you reading a bedtime story
while I listen in the hall.
This will be the first home
our children remember,
and I doubt they'll notice
if the floors aren't level.

Spare Bedrooms

Upstairs, the spare bedrooms wait
expectant, like the
constant comments

You've been married
long enough now,
time to start a family.

I wish that I could tell them
how desperately I want to see
the little bedrooms filled

how the emptiness devours me,
how their questions and their pressures
are the background of my nightmares

how they make me want to scream
"We're trying, and we don't know
if it will ever happen."

How much easier and harder
it is to smile and say,
"We haven't talked about it yet."

Uncertainty

When I try to imagine
what you will be like,
I get stuck in the hope
that you will be at all.

Positive

Fair food, fried and favored
turns in my stomach, treacherously
to the tinny candy carnival songs
and the chorus of the crowd.
A couple floats by,
overjoyed as the push their stroller.
I look away.
The doctors said
infertility was a side effect of the medication.
Not that it *couldn't* happen,
but that we should let them know
if it didn't.
And it hasn't.
The shouts and the music
and the smells of grease
and the cries of babies
chase me all the way back home.
I took a test last week
(negative)
and the thought of waiting another month seems
unbearable.
I can still smell the deep fried
promises of false comfort and
my stomach squirms again,
like a bottled message
tossed up on the shore.
I have to leave soon, but
I have time for a quick test.
I leave it on the counter,
prepare to wait,
to distract myself for the five endless minutes, and
glance down and
two bright blue lines
smile back.

New Love

I thought I loved you
when I read the positive
and was terrified to go to the doctor
in case it was false.
I thought I loved you
when I answered the phone
and the nurse said
"Congratulations!"
I thought I loved you
when I heard your heartbeat for the first time,
saw you waving on the screen
and couldn't stop crying.
I thought I loved you
when I felt your first kick,
your first fit of hiccups,
your first summersault.
I thought I loved you
when the doctor said
"One last push,"
and I heard your first cry,
when I looked up and saw
the tears in your daddy's eyes.
But I had no idea.
I had never known love
until you were pressed in my arms
and for the first time
I felt my heart beat
outside my body.

Like This

I wish I could keep you like this
peaceful, perfect,
protected.
I wish I could soothe
all your problems with singing,
some rocking,
a kiss on the cheek.

And all while you sleep,
each breath takes you farther
from unburdened dreams
to a future of worry,
of anger, of
hurt.

And happiness too,
which I know you will chase
with your joys and mistakes,
but I wish
I could keep you
like this.

Moments

"The first time you hear him
humming while he plays,"
my mom says,
"your heart will just melt."

If that's what happens
in those sweet little moments
when I don't think I could
possibly love him any more,

I doubt my heart
will last that long.

To My Son (Born in 2020)

I wanted to share the world with you,
the art, the music, the poetry,
stories of heroes and
courage and
love.

I wanted to give you
songs and opportunities,
philosophy and truth.

Instead you have isolation,
division,
calculated misunderstandings,
insults and stones thrown
with no care or consequence,
burning cities and
burning bridges.

I wanted to share the world with you.
Now I want only
to give you the tools
to change it.

To My Daughter (Two Years Later)

I will share my history with you,
there's no way around that.
I can't take away the German hips or crooked teeth,
the history of cancer and depression,
the addiction to poetry
that has plagued our house for generations.
But I promise to pay for your braces and therapy and
to get you a library card.

I will share my present with you.
I trace my hand over the flutters,
embrace the nausea, the backaches,
the fact that I can't take any medication
or eat sushi.
I sing to you in the shower and
talk out loud when I feel you listening,
and I promise that when you can do more than
kick for attention,
I will listen too.

I will share my future with you,
the hopes and the tools for facing despair,
because there's plenty, and it won't be gone
by the time you're here.
I will let you fail safely, so you can
figure out how to fly, and I will
watch from the ground as you soar to places
I was too afraid to reach.
And I will love you even if you do that all
from only the safety of your imagination.

Breastfeeding Outside the Tomah VA Hospital

Overhead the August sun
casts halos over vibrant green
verdant pastures growing
underneath the glowing
emerald canopy of leaves.

I walk between the pools of shade
to the circle honorary,
spangled banners flowing
in the breezes blowing
with my bouncing baby nursing in my arms.

We are silent in the sunshine,
with the flowers and the flags,
and I feel the summer slowing
in the golden moment, knowing
how the whole of summer can happen in a day.

A Pumpkin Cold Foam Colored Moon

A pumpkin cold foam colored moon
and clouds of ocean blue
(a suitably New England hue)
keep me company while I nurse
my 3 month old.

October cold
breezes pluck the fishing nets
that decorate the restaurant walk,
lobster traps and menu chalk.

I am outside again, looking
in through the window at the rest
of the family. It falls to my breast
(her meal is more important than mine)
to soothe my crying daughter.

The sounds of the water
and harbor are hidden
by highway traffic, high on the hill
where I join the lonely ranks of mothers
throughout history.

A consistory
of pacing, shushing shadows,
missing conversation for the sake
of the future cradled in our arms.

It's tempting to only feel
the wind, the ache in my back,
the things that I lack, until I look down and find
two blue moons waxing in me
that no one inside gets to see.

Lessons From My Father

Being strong
is easy as building a façade
and calcifying the flesh underneath,
easy as sweeping away the cobwebs
and leaving the spiders in the corner.
Easy as filling memories
with torn-out pages
and photobooks with
pasted smiles,
gilded sunsets and silhouettes
to hide the imperfections.
Easy as covering up your hurt
by lashing out at others,
building a mask with the
half-healed scar tissue
on your family's face.
It takes only a gentle sweep of paint
to be strong.

.

Lessons From My Mother

Being gentle
is hard as getting up
at 5 am to milk the cows,
hard as watching them
go to slaughter when they grow up.
Hard as seeing the wrinkles in
your parents' faces,
seeing the empty barn and
graying wood,
knowing that when it falls
it will never be rebuilt.
Hard as leaving
when you've been raised to plant your roots
and bloom in the worst of droughts.
When thunder rattles your bones and
quiets your mind, you learn
it takes the strength of a storm
to be gentle.

Superhero

I used to think my mom was a superhero,
unshakable, able to
soothe any fear or hurt.
She could do everything,
knew everything.
She was both the
rock on which I built my dreams
and the garden that made them beautiful.
The first time I saw her cry
I was terrified because
it had to be something
unimaginable
and I felt the first paralyzing
crush of helplessness.
Little by little
I started to see
the cracks in the illusion.
I saw her mistakes,
her regrets,
her sacrifices.
I listened when she apologized
and when she didn't,
felt when her words could
hurt as well as heal,
saw the depths of her
patience and love.
And I began to understand:
my mom is not a superhero.
She is human, and that makes her
so much more.

Gray Hair

A silver strand
upon my head,

a testament
to daily bread.

And what is more,
each added chore

provides more riches than before.

Scribbles, Rhymes, and Lima Beans

I wrote my first poem in first grade,
waiting for my mom to pick me up from school,
splashing in the late winter parking lot puddles.
I recited it proudly when I climbed in the car:
"Ishy-Slushy through the snow."
The words came to me as words come to every child,
tumbled, jumbled, and perfect.
A child doesn't need meter or metaphor;
the words themselves are magic.

I didn't know then
that poetry would become my
lifeline,
my canvas,
my connection.
It didn't matter if the rhymes were stretched,
if the rhythm wasn't quite right,
if all I had were a few lines
scribbled on the back of my hand.
Poetry was the friend that never got too busy
and didn't mind if I did.

And when the world rained on me,
my words went from
paper cup lima bean seeds on the windowsill
to gardens of
snapdragons, edelweiss, ivy
and weeds,
all growing together in harmony.

The Poem That Started It All

Ishy-slushy through the snow,
Ishy-slushy, go, go, go.

Ishy-slushy in the morn,
Ishy-slushy when I'm born.

Ishy-slushy, walk, now run,
Ishy-slushy til the day's done.

Ishy-slushy, time to sing,
no more snow, today is spring!

> *–The me when I was 6*
> *who never thought that words*
> *could be something worth critiquing.*
>
> *Words were simply joy.*

Acknowledgements

This book would not be possible without the blessings of God and the support of some amazing people. First of all, to my mother Donna and my brother Ramsay, who embraced my worst stories and pretended to like them anyway. To my friends, who enthusiastically shared in my excitement and let me ramble about my ideas, and especially to Brooke, the incredibly talented photographer who captured my headshots. And to my husband Michael, whose love, encouragement, and pancakes helped make this dream a reality. Thank you all.

About the Author

Rachael Waldburger is a lifelong writer and artist, as well as a regular consumer of fiction and caffeine. She lives in Wisconsin with her amazing husband, two wild children, and a pair of lazy cats. During the school year, she teaches middle school English and art. In the summer, she lives mostly in her stories.

For more information, go to rachaelwaldburger.com or follow Rachael on social media.

Facebook: Rachael Waldburger-Writer
Instagram: rachaelwaldburger
Twitter: @RewriteAgain

Sign up for Rachael's newsletter here: